Penmanship

Student Workbook

Author:
Mary Ellen Quint, Ph.D.

Editors:
Al Christopherson, Jessica Choi, Jennifer Davis, Kira Stout

Illustrators:
Craig Garrison, Mark Geyer, Robert Islas

Alpha Omega Publications, Inc.• Rock Rapids, IA

Horizons Penmanship 4 Student Workbook
© MMIV by Alpha Omega Publications, Inc.®
804 N. 2nd Ave. E., Rock Rapids, IA 51246-1759
All rights reserved.

No part of this publication may be reproduced, stored in an electronic retrieval system, or transmitted in any form by any means—electronic, mechanical, photocopy, recording, or otherwise—without the prior written permission of Alpha Omega Publications, Inc. Brief quotations may be used in literary review.

Scripture taken from the HOLY BIBLE, NEW INTERNATIONAL VERSION.
Copyright 1973, 1978, 1984 by the International Bible Society.
Used by permission of Zondervan® Publishing House.

Printed in the United States of America.

ISBN 978-0-7403-0747-8

Table of Contents

Introduction 2

Tips for Good Handwriting 3

Correct Formation of Manuscript Letters and Numbers 5

Correct Formation of Cursive Letters and Numbers 7

Parables in *Horizons Penmanship 4*

Jesus Speaks in Parables (Lessons 1–5) 9

The Parable of the Mustard Seed (Lessons 6–10) 15

The Parables of the Hidden Treasure and the Pearl (Lessons 11–15) 21

The Parable of the Lost Sheep (Lessons 16–20) 27

The Parable of the Lost Coin (Lessons 21–25) 35

The Parable of the Good Shepherd (Lessons 26–40) 41

The Parable of the Good Samaritan (Lessons 41–55) 59

The Parable of the Lost Son (Lessons 56–90) 77

The Parable of the Sower and the Seed (Lessons 91–110) 121

The Parable of the Pharisee and the Tax Collector (Lessons 111–120) 145

The Parable of the Weeds (Lessons 121–145) 157

The Parable of the Unmerciful Servant (Lessons 146–160) 187

Introduction

Welcome to *Horizons Penmanship* 4! Good handwriting is a necessary skill in life. Today, you may rely on computers to do a lot of writing, but the ability to fill in a form, to write a card of congratulations, or to write a personal letter to a friend using clearly formed letters is important. Like riding a bike or developing any other skill, handwriting must be learned and perfected through consistent practice. While *Horizons Penmanship 4* does not introduce any new letters or forms for you to learn, it does offer you a time of focused study to practice your writing. In this course, you will practice penmanship using parables from the Gospels.

Each week, you'll complete five lessons that will require you to practice penmanship by copying part or all of a new parable. Take a look at the brief description of the five lesson types below. This will help you prepare for your work in this course.

Day 1: Cursive Practice — You'll learn new vocabulary words related to the parable for the week. You'll also get to practice writing a few sentences to prepare you for thinking about the parable for the week.

Day 2: Cursive Practice — You'll practice cursive writing by answering some key questions about the parable. These questions will help you understand and share what you know about the parable.

Day 3: Manuscript Practice — Manuscript writing is important. On this day, you'll get to practice writing part or all of the parable using manuscript writing.

Day 4: Final Cursive Practice — On this day, you'll practice writing the entire parable for the week in cursive. This will help you practice for Day 5.

Day 5: Penmanship Performance — Now you're ready to demonstrate that practice makes perfect! On this day, you'll copy the parable for the week onto the specially designated page, using your best cursive handwriting. You can decorate all your penmanship performance pages and display them in a separate binder or booklet.

As you begin working through the lessons, you'll notice that there are guidelines in place to help you accurately place your writing on the page. These lines will gradually become smaller in size until they resemble the lined paper you use in school or for other work. Guidelines will be used in each lesson throughout the course until Lesson 122. After that, two lessons each week will not have guidelines. This will help you grow accustomed to writing on regular tablet paper.

Are you ready to polish your penmanship skills while learning the valuable lessons Jesus taught us? Grab your pencils and let's get started!

Tips for Good Handwriting

Correct Right-Handed Position

Correct Left-Handed Position

Paper is placed on an angle to the left. An arrow drawn on the bottom left-hand corner of the writing paper should point toward the belly button. Left hand steadies the paper and moves it up as you near the bottom of the page. Right hand is free to write. Their right arm should be at a right angle to the lines on the paper.

Correct Hand and Pencil Position

Hold the pencil loosely about 1/2" to 1" above the sharpened point. Hold it between your thumb and index (pointer) finger. Let it rest on your middle finger. Do not grip the pencil tightly, or your hand will become very tired. Do not let your hand slip down to the sharp point, or you will have difficulty writing properly. Keep the wrist rolled down toward the paper. Triangular pencil grips can be used to help develop correct finger positioning.

Left-handed students should hold the pencil loosely about 1" to 1 1/2" above the sharpened point.

Paper is placed at an angle of 30-45 degrees to the edge of the desk. An arrow drawn on the bottom right-hand corner of the writing paper should point toward the right shoulder of the student for manuscript writing and toward the belly for cursive writing. Right hand steadies the paper and moves it up as you near the bottom of the page. Left hand is free to write. Watch the hand positions carefully as shown in the picture. Books or other materials should be placed at the right of the paper.

Left-handed writers should never write on paper that is held in a three-ring binder. This may force the student to adopt a hook position. Lesson pages from the Horizons Penmanship student book should be removed for the same reason. Some experts recommend a table or desk that is two inches lower than the height used by a right-handed student.

Left-handed students should be seated on the right side of the room facing the board to better see demonstrations as they are performed.

Sit up tall, leaning slightly forward but not bending over your desk. Have your feet flat on the floor. Both arms will rest on the desk. Hold the paper with your free hand.

Correct Spacing

The space between cursive sentences should be a cursive uppercase *O*.

Draw an uppercase O between sentences.

Guide Lines

The blue top and bottom lines and the dotted red centerline will be your guides for letter formations. Some letters are one space tall, others are two spaces tall. Some letters, like a lowercase *p*, are two spaces tall but begin in the bottom space and drop down one space below the bottom guideline. A few letters, like the uppercase *Y*, are three spaces tall. They use both spaces between the guidelines and drop one space below the line.

Correct Formation of Manuscript Letters and Numbers

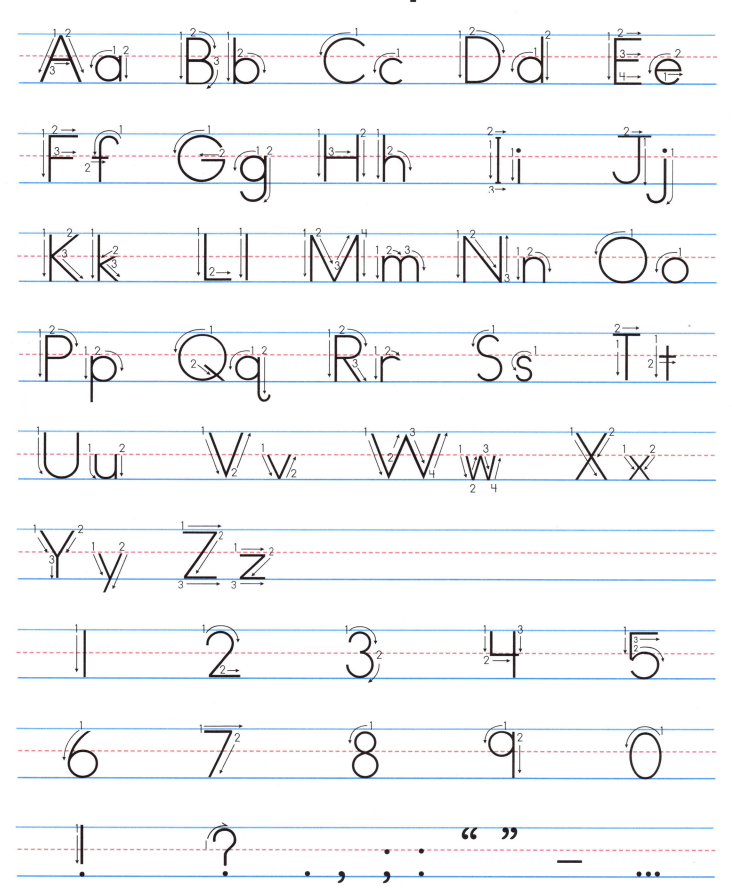

Horizons Penmanship 4

Correct Formation of Cursive Letters and Numbers

Aa Bb Cc Dd

Ee Ff Gg Hh

Ii Jj Kk Ll

Mm Nn Oo Pp

Qq Rr Ss Tt

Uu Vv Ww Xx

Yy Zz

1 2 3 4 5 6 7 8 9 0

! ? . , : ; " " — ...

Lesson 1: Jesus Speaks In Parables
Matthew 13:34–35

Name: _____

Cursive Practice: Trace and write the words on the lines.

Parable

Matthew

Use the blank lines to practice writing the sentences.

A parable is a story that teaches a lesson.

Jesus taught people with parables.

Parables still teach us lessons today.

What is your favorite parable?

You will write parables in Penmanship 4.

Lesson 2: Jesus Speaks In Parables
Matthew 13:34–35

Name: _____

Cursive Practice: Trace and write the words on the lines.

Gospel

kingdom

heaven

Use the blank lines to practice writing the sentences.

Some parables in the Gospels begin with,
"The kingdom of heaven is...

... like a pearl."

... like a net."

... like yeast."

The kingdom of heaven is within you.

Lesson 3 — Jesus Speaks In Parables
Matthew 13:34–35

Name: _____

Manuscript Practice: Use the blank lines to practice writing the sentences.

The kingdom of heaven is like a treasure.

The kingdom of heaven is like a man who sows seed.

The kingdom of heaven is like a mustard seed.

Jesus told parables to help us understand the kingdom of heaven.

Jesus told the parable of the Good Shepherd.

Jesus told the parable of the Good Samaritan.

Horizons Penmanship 4

Lesson 4 — Jesus Speaks In Parables — Matthew 13:34–35

Name: _____

Final Cursive Practice: Practice writing the parable on the lines below.

In Matthew 13:34–35, it says: "Jesus spoke all these things to the crowd in parables; he did not say anything to them without using a parable. So was fulfilled what was spoken through the prophet: 'I will open my mouth in parables, I will utter things hidden since the creation of the world.'"

Lesson 5: Jesus Speaks In Parables
Matthew 13:34–35

Name: _____

Penmanship Performance: Using the copy your teacher gives you, write the parable in your best cursive handwriting. *This lesson is continued on the next page.*

Lesson 5: Jesus Speaks In Parables
Matthew 13:34–35

Name: _____

You may decorate this page with a drawing of your own:

Lesson 6: The Parable of the Mustard Seed
Mark 4:30–32

Name: _____

Cursive Practice: Trace and write the words on the lines.

Mark 4:30–32

The Mustard Seed

Use the blank lines to practice writing the sentences.

A mustard seed is very small.

It is one of the smallest seeds.

Have you ever seen a mustard seed?

The kingdom of God is like the mustard seed?

Horizons Penmanship 4

Lesson 7: The Parable of the Mustard Seed
Mark 4:30–32

Name: _____

Cursive Practice: Trace and write the words on the lines.

largest

smallest

shade

branches

plant

birds

perch

Use the blank lines to practice writing the sentences.

It becomes the largest of all garden plants.

It is the smallest seed of all.

It has such big branches that the birds can perch in its shade.

Lesson 8: The Parable of the Mustard Seed
Mark 4:30–32

Name: _____

Manuscript Practice: Use the blank lines to practice writing the sentences.

In the gospels of Matthew, Mark, and Luke, Jesus uses the parable of the mustard seed to teach us about the kingdom of God.

In Mark 4:30–31, Jesus says, "What shall we say the kingdom of God is like, or what parable shall we use to describe it?"

It is like a mustard seed, which is the smallest seed you can plant in the ground.

Horizons Penmanship 4

Lesson 9: The Parable of the Mustard Seed
Mark 4:30–32

Name: _____

Final Cursive Practice: Using the copy your teacher gives you, practice writing the parable on the lines below.

Lesson 10

The Parable of the **Mustard Seed**
Mark 4:30–32

Name: _____

Penmanship Performance: Using the copy your teacher gives you, write the parable in your best cursive handwriting. *This lesson is continued on the next page.*

Lesson 10: The Parable of the Mustard Seed
Mark 4:30–32

Name: _____

What does this parable mean to you?

Lesson 11 — The Parable of the Hidden Treasure & The Pearl
Matthew 13:44–45

Name: _____

Cursive Practice: Trace and write the words on the lines. Define each word or use it in a sentence.

Treasure

Hidden

field

bought

Use the blank lines to copy and answer the question.

Have you ever found a "treasure"?

Use the blank lines to copy and answer the question. In your answer, explain why.

Have you ever hidden something?

Horizons Penmanship 4

Lesson 12
The Parable of the Hidden Treasure & The Pearl
Matthew 13:44–45

Name: _____

Cursive Practice: Trace and write the words on the lines. Define each word or use it in a sentence.

Joy

Luke

Use the blank lines to practice writing the sentence.

In Luke 17:21, Jesus tells us that "the kingdom of God is within you."

Use the blank lines to copy and answer the question.

Why is a hidden treasure so special?

Lesson 13 — **The Parable of the Hidden Treasure & The Pearl**
Matthew 13:44–45

Name:

Manuscript Practice: Trace and write the words on the lines. Define each word or use it in a sentence.

Pearl

everything

merchant

value

great

Use the blank lines to copy and answer the question in manuscript.

What has great value for you? Why?

Horizons Penmanship 4

Lesson 14

The Parable of the Hidden Treasure & The Pearl
Matthew 13:44–45

Name: _____

Final Cursive Practice: Using the copy your teacher gives you, practice writing the parable on the lines below.

Lesson 15: The Parable of the Hidden Treasure & The Pearl

Matthew 13:44–45

Name: _____

Penmanship Performance: Using the copy your teacher gives you, write the parable in your best cursive handwriting. *This lesson is continued on the next page.*

Lesson 15: The Parable of the Hidden Treasure & The Pearl
Matthew 13:44–45

Name: _____

What does this parable mean to you?

Lesson 16 —  Luke 15:3-7

Name: _____

Cursive Practice: Trace and write the words on the lines. Use the words in a sentence.

The Lost Sheep

hundred

ninety-nine

country

neighbors

Rejoice

shoulders

righteous

repent

Horizons Penmanship 4

Lesson 17: The Parable of the Lost Sheep

Luke 15:3–7

Name: _____

Cursive Practice: Use the blank lines to practice writing the sentences.

Suppose a man loses one of his sheep.

When he finds it, he joyfully puts it on his shoulders and goes home.

Rejoice with me.

There will be more rejoicing in heaven over one sinner who repents than over ninety-nine righteous who do not need to repent.

Lesson 19: The Parable of the Lost Sheep
Luke 15:3–7

Name: _____

Final Cursive Practice: Practice writing the parable on the lines below.
This lesson is continued on the next page.

Jesus told this parable: "Suppose one of you has a hundred sheep and loses one of them. Does he not leave the ninety-nine in the open country and go after the lost sheep until he finds it? And when he finds it, he joyfully puts it on his shoulders and goes home."

Lesson 19 — The Parable of the Lost Sheep (Luke 15:3–7)

Name: _____

"Then he calls his friends and neighbors together and says, 'Rejoice with me; I have found my lost sheep.' I tell you that in the same way there will be more rejoicing in heaven over one sinner who repents than over ninety-nine righteous persons who do not need to repent." Luke 15:3-7

Lesson 20: The Parable of the Lost Sheep
Luke 15:3–7

Name: _____

Penmanship Performance: Using the copy your teacher gives you, write the parable in your best cursive handwriting. *This lesson is continued on the next page.*

Horizons Penmanship 4

Lesson 20: The Parable of the Lost Sheep
Luke 15:3–7

Name: _____

What does this parable mean to you?

Lesson 21: The Parable of the Lost Coin
Luke 15:8–10

Name: _____

Cursive Practice: Trace and write the words on the lines. Define each word or use it in a sentence.

The Lost Coin

silver coins

woman

Does

lamp

sweep

search

carefully

friends

Lesson 22 — The Parable of the Lost Coin
Luke 15:8–10

Name: _____

Cursive Practice: Trace and write the words on the lines. Define each word or use it in a sentence.

together

found

presence

angels

Use the blank lines to practice writing the sentences.

Or suppose a woman has ten silver coins and loses one. Does she not light a lamp, sweep the house and search carefully until she finds it?

Lesson 23: The Parable of the Lost Coin
Luke 15:8–10

Name: _____

Manuscript Practice: Use the blank lines to practice writing the sentences.

And when she finds it, she calls her friends and neighbors together and says, "Rejoice with me; I have found my lost coin."

In the same way, I tell you, there is rejoicing in the presence of the angels of God over one sinner who repents.

Lesson 24: The Parable of the Lost Coin
Luke 15:8–10

Name: _____

Final Cursive Practice: Using the copy your teacher gives you, practice writing the parable on the lines below.

Lesson 25: The Parable of the Lost Coin

Luke 15:8–10

Name: _____

Penmanship Performance: Using the copy your teacher gives you, write the parable in your best cursive handwriting. *This lesson is continued on the next page.*

Horizons Penmanship 4

Lesson 25: The Parable of the Lost Coin
Luke 15:8–10

Name: _____

What does this parable mean to you?

Lesson 26: The Parable of the Good Shepherd, Part 1
John 10:11-13

Name: _____

Cursive Practice: Trace and write the words on the lines.

The Good Shepherd

John 10:11-13

I am the good shepherd.

Use the blank lines to practice writing the sentences.

The good shepherd lays down his life for his sheep.

The hired hand is not the shepherd who owns the sheep.

Horizons Penmanship 4

Lesson 27: The Parable of the Good Shepherd, Part 1
John 10:11-13

Name: _____

Cursive Practice: Use the blank lines to practice writing the sentences.

So when he sees the wolf coming, he abandons the sheep and runs away.

Then the wolf attacks the flock and scatters it.

The man runs away because he is a hired hand and cares nothing for the sheep.

Write a sentence or definition for the following word: *abandons*

Lesson 28: The Parable of the Good Shepherd, Part 1
John 10:11-13

Name: _____

Manuscript Practice: Use the blank lines to copy and answer the questions.

Who is the Good Shepherd referred to here?

What is a hired hand?

Who does the wolf stand for in this parable?

Horizons Penmanship 4

Lesson 29 — The Parable of the **Good Shepherd** Part 1 — *John 10:11–13*

Name:

Final Cursive Practice: Using the copy your teacher gives you, practice writing the parable on the lines below.

Lesson 30 — The Parable of the **Good Shepherd** Part 1 — John 10:11–13

Name: _____

Penmanship Performance: Using the copy your teacher gives you, write the parable in your best cursive handwriting. *This lesson is continued on the next page.*

Horizons Penmanship 4

Lesson 30: The Parable of the Good Shepherd, Part 1
John 10:11–13

Name: _____

Lesson 31: The Parable of the Good Shepherd, Part 2
John 10:14–16

Name: _____

Cursive Practice: Trace and write the words on the lines. Define each word or use it in a sentence.

Father

flock

sheep pen

listen

Use the blank lines to copy and answer the question.

How do you listen to the Good Shepherd's voice?

Horizons Penmanship 4

Lesson 32: The Parable of the Good Shepherd, Part 2
John 10:14–16

Name: _____

Cursive Practice: Use the blank lines to practice writing the sentence.

I know my sheep and my sheep know me.

Use the blank lines to copy and answer the questions.

Who are Jesus' sheep?

Use the blank lines to practice writing the sentences.

The Father knows me and I know the Father.

I lay down my life for the sheep.

I have other sheep that are not in this sheep pen.

Lesson 33: The Parable of the Good Shepherd, Part 2
John 10:14–16

Name: _____

Manuscript Practice: Use the blank lines to practice writing the sentence.

I must bring them also.

Use the blank lines to copy and answer the question.

How does the shepherd bring in the sheep?

Use the blank lines to practice writing the sentences.

They will listen to my voice.

There shall be one flock and one shepherd.

Horizons Penmanship 4

Lesson 34 — The Parable of the Good Shepherd, Part 2
John 10:14–16

Name: _____

Final Cursive Practice: Using the copy your teacher gives you, practice writing the parable on the lines below.

Lesson 35: The Parable of the Good Shepherd, Part 2
John 10:14–16

Name: _____

Penmanship Performance: Using the copy your teacher gives you, write the parable in your best cursive handwriting. *This lesson is continued on the next page.*

Lesson 35: The Parable of the Good Shepherd, Part 2
John 10:14–16

Name: _____

What does this part of the parable mean to you?

Lesson 36 — The Parable of the Good Shepherd: Conclusion
John 10:17–18

Name: _____

Cursive Practice: Trace and write the words on the lines. Define each word or use it in a sentence.

accord

authority

command

reason

Use the blank lines to copy and answer the question.

How did Jesus lay down his life?

Lesson 37: The Parable of the Good Shepherd — Conclusion
John 10:17–18

Name: _____

Cursive Practice: Use the blank lines to copy and answer the questions.

How did Jesus take up his life again?

What does "I lay it down of my own accord" mean?

What "authority" does Jesus have?

Lesson 38: The Parable of the Good Shepherd — Conclusion
John 10:17-18

Name: _____

Manuscript Practice: Use the blank lines to practice writing the parable.

"The reason my Father loves me is that I lay down my life—only to take it up again.

No one takes it from me, but I lay it down of my own accord.

I have authority to lay it down and authority to take it up again.

This command I received from my Father." John 10:17-18

Lesson 39 — The Parable of the **Good Shepherd** Conclusion — John 10:17–18

Name: _____

Final Cursive Practice: Using the copy your teacher gives you, practice writing the parable on the lines below.

Lesson 40 — The Parable of the Good Shepherd Conclusion — John 10:17–18

Name: _____

Penmanship Performance: Using the copy your teacher gives you, write the parable in your best cursive handwriting. *This lesson is continued on the next page.*

Lesson 40
The Parable of the Good Shepherd
Conclusion
John 10:17–18

Name:

What does this part of the parable mean to you?

Lesson 41: The Parable of the Good Samaritan, Part 1
Luke 10:30–32

Name: _____

Cursive Practice: Trace and write the words on the lines. Define each word or use it in a sentence.

The Good Samaritan

Jerusalem

Jericho

robbers

priest

Levite

clothes

happened

Lesson 42 — The Parable of the Good Samaritan, Part 1 — Luke 10:30–32

Name: _____

Cursive Practice: Use the blank lines to copy and answer the questions.

What did the robbers do to the man?

What did the priest do?

What did the Levite do?

What would you do?

Lesson 43: The Parable of the Good Samaritan, Part 1
Luke 10:30–32

Name: _____

Manuscript Practice: Use the blank lines to practice writing the sentences.

A man was going down from Jerusalem to Jericho, when he fell into the hands of robbers.

They stripped him of his clothes, beat him and went away, leaving him half dead.

A priest happened to be going down the same road, and when he saw the man, he passed by on the other side.

Horizons Penmanship 4

Name: _____

Final Cursive Practice: Using the copy your teacher gives you, practice writing the parable on the lines below.

Lesson 45: The Parable of the Good Samaritan, Part 1

Luke 10:30–32

Name: _____

Penmanship Performance: Using the copy your teacher gives you, write the parable in your best cursive handwriting. *This lesson is continued on the next page.*

Lesson 45: The Parable of the Good Samaritan, Part 1
Luke 10:30–32

Name: _____

What does this part of the parable mean to you?

Lesson 46: The Parable of the Good Samaritan, Part 2
Luke 10:33–34

Name: _____

Cursive Practice: Trace and write the words on the lines. Define each word or use it in a sentence.

Samaritan

traveled

pity

bandaged

wounds

inn

Use the blank lines to answer the question.

How was the Samaritan different from the priest and the Levite?

Horizons Penmanship 4

Lesson 47 — The Parable of the Good Samaritan, Part 2 (Luke 10:33–34)

Name:

Cursive Practice: Use the blank lines to practice writing the sentences.

But a Samaritan, as he traveled, came where the man was;

and when he saw him, he took pity on him.

He went to him and bandaged his wounds, pouring on oil and wine.

Then he put the man on his own donkey, took him to an inn, and took care of him.

Lesson 48 — The Parable of the Good Samaritan Part 2 — Luke 10:33–34

Name: _____

Manuscript Practice: Use the blank lines to practice writing the sentences.

But a Samaritan, as he traveled, came where the man was; and when he saw him, he took pity on him.

He went to him and bandaged his wounds, pouring on oil and wine.

Then he put the man on his own donkey, took him to an inn and took care of him.

Horizons Penmanship 4

Lesson 49: The Parable of the Good Samaritan, Part 2

Luke 10:33–34

Name: _____

Final Cursive Practice: Using the copy your teacher gives you, practice writing the parable on the lines below.

Lesson 50 — The Parable of the Good Samaritan, Part 2
Luke 10:33–34

Name: _____

Penmanship Performance: Using the copy your teacher gives you, write the parable in your best cursive handwriting. *This lesson is continued on the next page.*

Lesson 50: The Parable of the Good Samaritan, Part 2
Luke 10:33–34

Name: _____

What does this part of the parable mean to you?

You may decorate this page with a drawing of your own:

Lesson 51: The Parable of the Good Samaritan — Conclusion (Luke 10:35–37)

Name: _____

Cursive Practice: Trace and write the words on the lines. Define each word or use it in a sentence.

reimburse

innkeeper

expense

expert

mercy

Use the blank lines to answer the questions.

What question did Jesus ask?

What did the law expert answer?

Horizons Penmanship 4

Lesson 52: The Parable of the Good Samaritan — Conclusion
Luke 10:35–37

Name: _____

Cursive Practice: Use the blank lines to copy and answer the questions.

What does "Go and do likewise" mean to you?

How can you be a Good Samaritan?

Horizons Penmanship 4

Lesson 53: The Parable of the Good Samaritan — Conclusion
Luke 10:35–37

Name: _____

Manuscript Practice: Use the blank lines to practice writing the sentences.

The next day he took out two silver coins and gave them to the innkeeper.

"Look after him," he said, "and when I return, I will reimburse you for any extra expense you may have."

Which of these three do you think was a neighbor to the man who fell into the hands of robbers?

The expert in the law replied, "The one who had mercy on him."

Jesus told him, "Go and do likewise."

Horizons Penmanship 4

Lesson 54 — The Parable of the Good Samaritan, Conclusion (Luke 10:35–37)

Name: _____

Final Cursive Practice: Using the copy your teacher gives you, practice writing the parable on the lines below.

Lesson 55: The Parable of the Good Samaritan — Conclusion
Luke 10:35–37

Name: _____

Penmanship Performance: Using the copy your teacher gives you, write the parable in your best cursive handwriting. *This lesson is continued on the next page.*

Lesson 55: The Parable of the Good Samaritan — Conclusion
Luke 10:35–37

Name: _____

What does this part of the parable mean to you?

Lesson 56 Part 1: The Parable of the Lost Son
Luke 15:11–13

Name: _____

Cursive Practice: Trace and write the words on the lines. Define or use the words in a sentence.

The Lost Son

share

estate

divided

property

distant

squandered

wealth

younger

Horizons Penmanship 4

Lesson 57 — The Parable of the Lost Son, Part 1
Luke 15:11-13

Name: _____

Cursive Practice: Use the blank lines to copy and answer the questions.

How many sons did the man have?

What did the younger son ask for?

What did the father do?

What did the younger son do with his money.

Name: _____

Manuscript Practice: Use the blank lines to practice writing the parable.

The Lost Son

"...There was a man who had two sons. The younger one said to his father, 'Father, give me my share of the estate.' So he divided his property between them. Not long after, the younger son got together all he had, set off for a distant country and there squandered his wealth in wild living." Luke 15:11-13

Horizons Penmanship 4

Lesson 59 — The Parable of the Lost Son (Part 1, Luke 15:11-13)

Name: _____

Final Cursive Practice: Using the copy your teacher gives you, practice writing the parable on the lines below.

Lesson 60 — The Parable of the Lost Son, Part 1
Luke 15:11–13

Name: _____

Penmanship Performance: Using the copy your teacher gives you, write the parable in your best cursive handwriting. *This lesson is continued on the next page.*

Horizons Penmanship 4

Lesson 60 — The Parable of the Lost Son, Part 1
Luke 15:11–13

Name: _____

What does this part of the parable mean to you?

Lesson 61 — The Parable of the Lost Son
Part 2 — Luke 15:14–16

Name: _____

Cursive Practice: Trace and write the words on the lines. Define each word or use it in a sentence.

severe

famine

citizen

whole

longed

stomach

In your own words, retell Part 1 of the Parable of the Lost Son.

Horizons Penmanship 4

Lesson 62 — The Parable of the Lost Son
Part 2 — Luke 15:14–16

Name: _____

Cursive Practice: Use the blank lines to copy and answer the questions. Use complete sentences.

What happened to the son after he spent all his money?

What did he do to survive after his money was gone?

Did anyone help him?

What do you think he should do now?

Lesson 63 Part 2 — The Parable of the Lost Son
Luke 15:14–16

Name: _____

Manuscript Practice: Use the blank lines to practice writing the sentences.

After he had spent everything, there was a severe famine in that whole country, and he began to be in need.

So he went and hired himself out to a citizen of that country, who sent him to the fields to feed the pigs.

He longed to fill his stomach with the pods that the pigs were eating, but no one gave him anything.

Lesson 64 Part 2: The Parable of the Lost Son
Luke 15:14–16

Name: _____

Final Cursive Practice: Using the copy your teacher gives you, practice writing the parable on the lines below.

Lesson 65 Part 2: The Parable of the Lost Son
Luke 15:14–16

Name: _____

Penmanship Performance: Using the copy your teacher gives you, write the parable in your best cursive handwriting. *This lesson is continued on the next page.*

Horizons Penmanship 4

Lesson 65 Part 2: The Parable of the Lost Son
Luke 15:14-16

Name: _____

What does this part of the parable mean to you?

88   Horizons Penmanship 4

Lesson 66 — The Parable of the Lost Son, Part 3 (Luke 15:17-19)

Name: _____

Cursive Practice: Trace and write the words on the lines. Define each word or use it in a sentence.

senses

starving

death

sinned

heaven

worthy

longer

Trace the question, then use the blank lines to answer the question. Be sure to use complete sentences.

What was the son going to do?

Lesson 67 — The Parable of the Lost Son, Part 3 (Luke 15:17–19)

Name: _____

Cursive Practice: Use the blank lines to copy and answer the questions. Use complete sentences.

What did the younger son remember about his father's servants?

What did he decide to do?

What did he plan to say to his father?

Horizons Penmanship 4

Lesson 68 Part 3: The Parable of the Lost Son
Luke 15:17-19

Name: _____

Manuscript Practice: Use the blank lines to practice writing the sentences.

When he came to his senses, he said, "How many of my father's hired men have food to spare, and here I am starving to death!

I will set out and go back to my father and say to him: Father, I have sinned against heaven and against you.

I am no longer worthy to be called your son; make me like one of your hired men."

Lesson 69 — The Parable of the Lost Son (Part 3, Luke 15:17–19)

Name: _____

Final Cursive Practice: Using the copy your teacher gives you, practice writing the parable on the lines below.

Lesson 70 Part 3

The Parable of the Lost Son
Luke 15:17–19

Name: _____

Penmanship Performance: Using the copy your teacher gives you, write the parable in your best cursive handwriting. *This lesson is continued on the next page.*

Horizons Penmanship 4

Lesson 70 Part 3
The Parable of the Lost Son
Luke 15:17–19

Name: _____

What does this part of the parable mean to you?

Horizons Penmanship 4

Lesson 71 — The Parable of the Lost Son
Part 4 — Luke 15:20–21

Name: _____

Cursive Practice: Trace and write the word on the lines. Define the word or use it in a sentence.

compassion

Use the blank lines to answer the questions.

What did the father do when he saw his son?

What did the son say to his father?

What do you think the father will do?

Horizons Penmanship 4

Lesson 72 — The Parable of the Lost Son, Part 4
Luke 15:20–21

Name: _____

Cursive Practice: Use the blank lines to answer the questions. Use complete sentences.

What do you do when you have hurt your parents or a friend?

How do you act toward someone who has hurt you?

Who is like the father in the story and will always forgive us?

Lesson 73 — The Parable of the Lost Son, Part 4
Luke 15:20–21

Name: _____

Manuscript Practice: Use the blank lines to practice writing the parable.

"So he got up and went to his father. But while he was still a long way off, his father saw him and was filled with compassion for him; he ran to his son, threw his arms around him and kissed him.

The son said to him, 'Father, I have sinned against heaven and against you. I am no longer worthy to be called your son.'" Luke 15:20–21

Horizons Penmanship 4

Lesson 74 — The Parable of the Lost Son
Part 4 • Luke 15:20–21

Name: _____

Final Cursive Practice: Using the copy your teacher gives you, practice writing the parable on the lines below.

Lesson 75

The Parable of the Lost Son Part 4
Luke 15:20–21

Name:

Penmanship Performance: Using the copy your teacher gives you, write the parable in your best cursive handwriting. *This lesson is continued on the next page.*

Lesson 75 — The Parable of the Lost Son
Part 4 — Luke 15:20–21

Name: _____

What does this part of the parable mean to you?

Lesson 76 — The Parable of the Lost Son
Part 5 — Luke 15:22–24

Name: _____

Cursive Practice: Trace and write the words on the lines. Define each word or use it in a sentence.

servants

sandals

fattened calf

feast

celebrate

alive

Quick!

Let's

Bring

Horizons Penmanship 4

Lesson 77 — The Parable of the Lost Son
Part 5 — Luke 15:22-24

Name: _____

Cursive Practice: Use the blank lines to answer the questions. Use complete sentences.

What did the father do?

What did the father mean when he said that his son was dead and is now alive?

What other parables talked about lost things being found?

Lesson 78 — The Parable of the Lost Son, Part 5

Luke 15:22–24

Name: _____

Manuscript Practice: Use the blank lines to practice writing the parable.

"The father said to his servants, 'Quick! Bring the best robe and put it on him. Put a ring on his finger and sandals on his feet. Bring the fattened calf and kill it. Let's have a feast and celebrate. For this son of mine was dead and is now alive; he was lost and is found.' So they began to celebrate." Luke 15:22–24

Lesson 79 — The Parable of the Lost Son
Part 5 · Luke 15:22–24

Name: _____

Final Cursive Practice: Using the copy your teacher gives you, practice writing the parable on the lines below.

Lesson 80 Part 5 — The Parable of the Lost Son
Luke 15:22–24

Name: _____

Penmanship Performance: Using the copy your teacher gives you, write the parable in your best cursive handwriting. *This lesson is continued on the next page.*

Lesson 80: The Parable of the Lost Son — Part 5
Luke 15:22–24

Name: _____

What does this part of the parable mean to you?

Lesson 81: The Parable of the Lost Son, Part 6
Luke 15:25–28a

Name: _____

Cursive Practice: Trace and write the words on the lines. Define each word or use it in a sentence.

Meanwhile

older

music

dancing

angry

refused

Use the blank lines to answer the question.

Why was the older son angry?

Horizons Penmanship 4

Lesson 82

Cursive Practice: Use the blank lines to copy and answer the questions. Use complete sentences.

What did the older son hear as he came home?

What did he ask the servant?

What did the servant answer?

What did the older brother refuse to do?

Lesson 83 — The Parable of the Lost Son
Part 6 — Luke 15:25–28a

Name: _____

Manuscript Practice: Use the blank lines to practice writing the parable.

"Meanwhile, the older son was in the field. When he came near the house, he heard music and dancing. So he called one of the servants and asked him what was going on. 'Your brother has come,' he replied, 'and your father has killed the fattened calf because he has him back safe and sound.' The older brother became angry and refused to go in."

Luke 15:25–28a

Lesson 84 — The Parable of the Lost Son
Part 6 — Luke 15:25–28a

Name: _____

Final Cursive Practice: Using the copy your teacher gives you, practice writing the parable on the lines below.

Name: _____

Penmanship Performance: Using the copy your teacher gives you, write the parable in your best cursive handwriting. *This lesson is continued on the next page.*

Lesson 85 Part 6: The Parable of the Lost Son
Luke 15:25–28a

Name: _____

What does this part of the parable mean to you?

Lesson 86 — **The Parable of the Lost Son** Conclusion — Luke 15:28b–31

Name: _____

Cursive Practice: Trace and write the words on the lines. Define each word or use it in a sentence.

pleaded

answered

slaving

disobeyed

never

Use the blank lines to answer the question.

Why did the father say they needed to celebrate?

Horizons Penmanship 4

Lesson 87: The Parable of the Lost Son — Conclusion
Luke 15:28b–31

Name: _____

Cursive Practice: Use the blank lines to copy and answer the questions.

What did the father do about the older son?

Why did the older son say he was angry?

Who said, "You are always with me and everything I have is yours"?

Name: _____

Manuscript Practice: Practice writing the parable on the lines below. *This lesson is continued on the next page.*

"So his father went out and pleaded with him. But he answered his father, 'Look! All these years I've been slaving for you and never disobeyed your orders. Yet you never gave me even a young goat so I could celebrate with my friends. But when this son of yours who has squandered your property…comes home, you kill the fattened calf for him!'

Lesson 88: The Parable of the Lost Son — Conclusion (Luke 15:28b–31)

'My son,' the father said, 'you are always with me, and everything I have is yours. But we had to celebrate and be glad because this brother of yours was dead and is alive again; he was lost and is found.'" Luke 15:28b–31

Lesson 89: The Parable of the Lost Son — Conclusion
Luke 15:28b–31

Name: _____

Final Cursive Practice: Using the copy your teacher gives you, practice writing the parable on the lines below. *This lesson is continued on the next page.*

Lesson 89: The Parable of the Lost Son — Conclusion

Luke 15:28b–31

Name: _____

You may decorate this page with a drawing of your own:

Lesson 90: The Parable of the Lost Son — Conclusion
Luke 15:28b–31

Name: _____

Penmanship Performance: Using the copy your teacher gives you, write the parable in your best cursive handwriting. *This lesson is continued on the next page.*

Horizons Penmanship 4

Lesson 90: The Parable of the Lost Son — Conclusion
Luke 15:28b–31

Name: _____

What does this part of the parable mean to you?

Lesson 91

The Parable of the Sower & the Seed Part 1
Luke 8:4–6

Name: _____

Cursive Practice: Trace and write the words on the lines. Define each word or use it in a sentence.

The Sower and the Seed

crowd

gathering

sower

scattering

trampled

withered

moisture

plants

Lesson 92 — The Parable of the Sower & the Seed, Part 1

Luke 8:4–6

Name: _____

Cursive Practice: Use the blank lines to answer the questions. Use complete sentences.

To whom was Jesus speaking when he told this parable?

What did the farmer go out to do?

What happened to the seed along the path?

Where else did some of the seed fall?

What happened to the seed that fell on rock?

Lesson 93 — The Parable of the Sower & the Seed, Part 1
Luke 8:4–6

Name: _____

Manuscript Practice: Use the blank lines to practice writing the parable.

The Sower and the Seed

While a large crowd was gathering, Jesus told them this parable: "A farmer went out to sow his seed. As he was scattering the seed, some fell along the path; it was trampled on, and the birds ate it up. Some fell on rock, and when it came up, the plants withered because they had no moisture."

Luke 8:4–6

Lesson 94 — The Parable of the Sower & the Seed, Part 1 — Luke 8:4–6

Name:

Final Cursive Practice: Practice writing the parable on the lines below.

The Sower and the Seed

While a large crowd was gathering, Jesus told them this parable: "A farmer went out to sow his seed. As he was scattering the seed, some fell along the path; it was trampled on, and the birds ate it up. Some fell on rock, and when it came up, the plants withered because they had no moisture."

Luke 8:4–6

Lesson 95: The Parable of the Sower & the Seed, Part 1
Luke 8:4–6

Name: _____

Penmanship Performance: Using the copy your teacher gives you, write the parable in your best cursive handwriting. *This lesson is continued on the next page.*

Lesson 95: The Parable of the Sower & the Seed Part 1
Luke 8:4–6

Name: _____

What does this part of the parable mean to you?

Lesson 96: The Parable of the Sower & the Seed, Part 2
Luke 8:7–9

Name: _____

Cursive Practice: Trace and write the words on the lines. Define each word or use it in a sentence.

thorns

choked

death

yielded

soil

Use the blank lines to answer the question.

What do you think Jesus meant when he said, "He who has ears to hear, let him hear"?

Horizons Penmanship 4

Lesson 97: The Parable of the Sower & the Seed, Part 2
Luke 8:7–9

Name: _____

Cursive Practice: Use the blank lines to answer the questions.

What happened to the seeds that fell in the thorns?

What happened to the seeds that fell on good soil?

What did Jesus call out when he finished the parable?

Did the disciples understand the parable?

Lesson 98 — The Parable of the Sower & the Seed, Part 2 — Luke 8:7–9

Name: _____

Manuscript Practice: Use the blank lines to practice writing the sentences.

Other seed fell among thorns, which grew up with it and choked the plants.

Still other seed fell on good soil.

It came up and yielded a crop, a hundred times more than was sown.

When he said this, he called out, "He who has ears to hear, let him hear."

His disciples asked him what this parable meant.

Horizons Penmanship 4

Lesson 99: The Parable of the Sower & the Seed, Part 2 — Luke 8:7–9

Name: _____

Final Cursive Practice: Practice writing the parable on the lines below.

"Other seed fell among thorns, which grew up with it and choked the plants. Still other seed fell on good soil. It came up and yielded a crop, a hundred times more than was sown."

"When he said this, he called out, 'He who has ears to hear, let him hear.'"

"His diciples asked him what this parable meant."

Luke 8:7–9

Lesson 100 — The Parable of the Sower & the Seed Part 2 — Luke 8:7–9

Name: _____

Penmanship Performance: Using the copy your teacher gives you, write the parable in your best cursive handwriting. *This lesson is continued on the next page.*

Lesson 101: The Parable of the Sower & the Seed, Part 3

Luke 8:11–13

Name: _____

Cursive Practice: Trace and write the words on the lines. Define each word or use it in a sentence.

The

This

They

Those

believe

testing

word of God

meaning

devil

Horizons Penmanship 4

Lesson 102: The Parable of the Sower & the Seed — Part 3
Luke 8:11-13

Name: _____

Cursive Practice: Use the blank lines to answer the questions.

What did Jesus say the seed was?

Who are the ones along the path?

What did Jesus say about the ones on the rocks?

Lesson 103: The Parable of the Sower & the Seed — Part 3
Luke 8:11-13

Name: _____

Manuscript Practice: Use the blank lines to practice writing the parable.

"This is the meaning of the parable:

The seed is the word of God. Those along the path are the ones who hear, and then the devil comes and takes away the word from their hearts so that they may not believe and be saved.

Those on the rock are the ones who receive the word with joy when they hear it, but they have no root. They believe for a while, but in the time of testing they fall away." Luke 8:11-13

Name: _____

Final Cursive Practice: Using the copy your teacher gives you, practice writing the parable on the lines below.

You may decorate this page with a drawing of your own:

Lesson 105

The Parable of the Sower & the Seed
Part 3
Luke 8:11–13

Name: _____

Penmanship Performance: Using the copy your teacher gives you, write the parable in your best cursive handwriting. *This lesson is continued on the next page.*

Lesson 105: The Parable of the Sower & the Seed — Part 3
Luke 8:11–13

Name: _____

What does this part of the parable mean to you?

Lesson 106: The Parable of the Sower & the Seed — Conclusion
Luke 8:14–15

Name: _____

Cursive Practice: Trace and write the words on the lines. Define each word or use it in a sentence.

worries

riches

pleasures

mature

noble

retain

persevering

produce

crop

Horizons Penmanship 4

Lesson 107: The Parable of the Sower & the Seed — Conclusion
Luke 8:14–15

Name: _____

Cursive Practice: Use the blank lines to answer the questions.

What did Jesus say about the seed that fell among the thorns?

What did Jesus say about the seed that fell on good soil?

Lesson 108

Name: _____

Manuscript Practice: Use the blank lines to practice writing the parable.

"The seed that fell among thorns stands for those who hear, but as they go on their way they are choked by life's worries, riches, and pleasures, and they do not mature. But the seed on good soil stands for those with a noble and good heart, who hear the word, retain it, and by persevering produce a crop." Luke 8:14-15

Lesson 109: The Parable of the Sower & the Seed — Conclusion
Luke 8:14-15

Name: _____

Final Cursive Practice: Practice writing the parable on the lines below.

"The seed that fell among thorns stands for those who hear, but as they go on their way they are choked by life's worries, riches, and pleasures, and they do not mature. But the seed on good soil stands for those with a noble and good heart, who hear the word, retain it, and by persevering produce a crop." Luke 8:14-15

Lesson 110

The Parable of the Sower & the Seed Conclusion
Luke 8:14–15

Name:

Penmanship Performance: Using the copy your teacher gives you, write the parable in your best cursive handwriting. *This lesson is continued on the next page.*

Horizons Penmanship 4

Lesson 110: The Parable of the Sower & the Seed — Conclusion
Luke 8:14–15

What does this part of the parable mean to you?

Lesson 111: The Parable of the Pharisee & the Tax Collector, Part 1

Luke 18:9b–12

Name: _____

Cursive Practice: Trace and write the words on the lines. Define each word or use it in a sentence.

Pharisee

Tax Collector

temple

prayed

himself

robbers

evildoers

twice

tenth

Lesson 112: The Parable of the Pharisee & the Tax Collector — Part 1

Luke 18:9b–12

Name: _____

Cursive Practice: Use the blank lines to answer the questions.

In Jesus' parable, how many men went to the temple to pray?

Who were the two men?

What did the Pharisee pray about himself?

Horizons Penmanship 4

Lesson 113 — The Parable of the Pharisee & the Tax Collector, Part 1 — Luke 18:9b–12

Name: _____

Manuscript Practice: Use the blank lines to practice writing the parable.

The Pharisee and the Tax Collector

Jesus told this parable: "Two men went up to the temple to pray, one a Pharisee and the other a tax collector.

The Pharisee prayed about himself: 'God, I thank you that I am not like other men—robbers, evildoers, adulterers—or even like this tax collector. I fast twice a week and give a tenth of all I get.'" Luke 18:9b–12

Horizons Penmanship 4

Lesson 114

The Parable of the Pharisee & the Tax Collector
Part 1
Luke 18:9b–12

Name: _____

Final Cursive Practice: Practice writing the parable on the lines below.

The Pharisee and the Tax Collector

Jesus told this parable: "Two men went up to the temple to pray, one a Pharisee and the other a tax collector. The Pharisee prayed about himself: 'God, I thank you that I am not like other men—robbers, evildoers, adulters—or even like this tax collector. I fast twice a week and give a tenth of all I get.'" Luke 18:9b–12

Lesson 115

The Parable of the Pharisee & the Tax Collector
Part 1
Luke 18:9b–12

Name:

Penmanship Performance: Using the copy your teacher gives you, write the parable in your best cursive handwriting. *This lesson is continued on the next page.*

Horizons Penmanship 4

Lesson 115: The Parable of the Pharisee & the Tax Collector
Part 1
Luke 18:9b–12

Name: _____

What does this part of the parable mean to you?

Lesson 116 — The Parable of the Pharisee & the Tax Collector — Conclusion — Luke 18:13–14

Name:

Cursive Practice: Trace and write the words on the lines. Define each word or use it in a sentence.

distance

beat

justified

exalts

humbles

rather

everyone

Use the blank lines to copy and answer the question.

Which man's prayer pleased God?

Cursive Practice: Use the blank lines to answer the questions.

Where was the tax collector standing?

What was he doing?

What was the tax collector's prayer?

Which man went home justified before God?

What lesson was Jesus teaching in this parable?

Horizons Penmanship 4

Lesson 118: The Parable of the Pharisee & the Tax Collector — Conclusion

Luke 18:13–14

Name: _____

Manuscript Practice: Use the blank lines to practice writing the parable.

"But the tax collector stood at a distance. He would not even look up to heaven, but beat his breast and said, 'God, have mercy on me, a sinner.'

"I tell you that this man, rather than the other, went home justified before God.

For everyone who exalts himself will be humbled, and he who humbles himself will be exalted." Luke 18:13-14

Lesson 119 — Luke 18:13-14

Name: _____

Final Cursive Practice: Practice writing the parable on the lines below.

"But the tax collector stood at a distance. He would not even look up to heaven, but beat his breast and said, 'God, have mercy on me, a sinner.'"

"Jesus said: 'I tell you that this man, rather than the other, went home justified before God. For everyone who exalts himself will be humbled, and he who humbles himself will be exalted.'"

Luke 18:13-14

Lesson 120: The Parable of the Pharisee & the Tax Collector — Conclusion
Luke 18:13–14

Name: _____

Penmanship Performance: Using the copy your teacher gives you, write the parable in your best cursive handwriting. *This lesson is continued on the next page.*

Lesson 120: The Parable of the Pharisee & the Tax Collector
Conclusion
Luke 18:13-14

Name: _____

What does this part of the parable mean to you?

Lesson 121 — The Parable of the Weeds, Part 1
Matthew 13:24–26

Name: _____

Cursive Practice: Trace and write the words on the lines. Define each word or use it in a sentence.

The Parable of the Weeds

sprouted

formed

appeared

Use the blank lines to answer the questions.

What other parable talks about a man sowing seeds?

What is different about this parable?

Horizons Penmanship 4

Lesson 122 — The Parable of the Weeds (Part 1)
Matthew 13:24–26

Name: _____

Cursive Practice: Use the blank lines to answer the questions.

To what does Jesus compare the kingdom of heaven in this parable?

Jesus compares

What happened while everyone was sleeping?

What happened when the wheat sprouted?

How do you think the man felt when he saw the weeds?

Horizons Penmanship 4

Lesson 123 — The Parable of the Weeds, Part 1
Matthew 13:24–26

Name: _____

Manuscript Practice: Use the blank lines to practice writing the parable.

The Parable of the Weeds

The Parable of the Weeds

Jesus told them another parable: "The kingdom of heaven is like a man who sowed good seed in his fields.

Jesus told them another

But while everyone was sleeping, his enemy came and sowed weeds among the wheat, and went away.

But while everyone

When the wheat sprouted and formed heads, then the weeds also appeared." Matthew 13:24–26

When the wheat

Horizons Penmanship 4

Final Cursive Practice: Practice writing the parable on the lines below.

The Parable of the Weeds

Jesus told them another parable: "The kingdom of heaven is like a man who sowed good seed in his fields. But while everyone was sleeping, his enemy came and sowed weeds among the wheat, and went away. When the wheat sprouted and formed heads, then the weeds also appeared."

Matthew 13:24–26

Lesson 125 Part 1

The Parable of the Weeds

Matthew 13:24–26

Name:

Penmanship Performance: Using the copy your teacher gives you, write the parable in your best cursive handwriting. *This lesson is continued on the next page.*

Lesson 125 — The Parable of the Weeds
Part 1 — Matthew 13:24–26

Name:

What does this part of the parable mean to you?

Name: _____

Cursive Practice: Trace and write the words on the lines. Define each word or use it in a sentence.

owner

servants

sir

Where

answered

pulling

root

Use the blank lines to answer the question.

Why did the owner tell his servants not to pull the weeds?

Horizons Penmanship Grade Four

Lesson 127 Part 2

Matthew 13:27-29

Name: _____

Cursive Practice: Use the blank lines to answer the questions.

Who came to the man and told him about the weeds?

What did the servants ask the man?

What was his answer?

What do you think the weeds stand for in this story?

Lesson 128 — The Parable of the Weeds, Part 2
Matthew 13:27–29

Name: _____

Manuscript Practice: Use the blank lines to practice writing the parable.

"The owner's servants came to him and said, 'Sir, didn't you sow good seed in your field? Where then did the weeds come from?'

'An enemy did this,' he replied.

"The servants asked him, 'Do you want us to go and pull them up?'

'No,' he answered, 'because while you are pulling the weeds, you may root up the wheat with them.'"

Matthew 13:27–29

Lesson 129 — The Parable of the Weeds, Part 2, Matthew 13:27-29

Name: _____

Final Cursive Practice: Practice writing the parable on the lines below.

"The owner's servants came to him and said, 'Sir, didn't you sow good seed in your field? Where then did the weeds come from?'
'An enemy did this,' he replied.
"The servants asked him, 'Do you want us to go and pull them up?'
'No,' he answered, 'because while you are pulling the weeds, you may root up the wheat with them.'" Matthew 13:27-29

Lesson 130 Part 2: The Parable of the Weeds
Matthew 13:27–29

Name: _____

Penmanship Performance: Using the copy your teacher gives you, write the parable in your best cursive handwriting. *This lesson is continued on the next page.*

Horizons Penmanship Grade Four

Lesson 130 Part 2 — The Parable of the Weeds — Matthew 13:27–29

Name: _____

What does this part of the parable mean to you?

You may decorate this page with a drawing of your own:

Lesson 131 — The Parable of the Weeds, Part 3
Matthew 13:30, 34

Name:

Cursive Practice: Trace and write the words on the lines. Define each word or use it in a sentence.

weeds

wheat

harvest

harvesters

collect

bundles

burned

gather

barn

together

anything

crowd

Horizons Penmanship Grade Four

Lesson 132 — The Parable of the Weeds (Part 3)
Matthew 13:30, 34

Cursive Practice: Use the blank lines to answer the questions.

How long did the man let the weeds and wheat grow?

What did he tell the harvesters to do with the weeds?

What did he tell them to do with the wheat?

How did Jesus speak to the crowd?

Lesson 133 — The Parable of the Weeds, Part 3
Matthew 13:30, 34

Name:

Manuscript Practice: Use the blank lines to practice writing the parable.

"'Let both [weeds and wheat] grow together until the harvest. At that time I will tell the harvesters: First collect the weeds and tie them in bundles to be burned; then gather the wheat and bring it into my barn.'"

"Jesus spoke all these things to the crowd in parables; he did not say anything to them without using a parable." Matthew 13:30, 34

Lesson 134 Part 3: The Parable of the Weeds

Matthew 13:30, 34

Name: _____

Final Cursive Practice: Practice writing the parable on the lines below.

"'Let both [weeds and wheat] grow together until the harvest. At that time I will tell the harvesters: First collect the weeds and tie them in bundles to be burned; then gather the wheat and bring it into my barn.'"

"Jesus spoke all these things to the crowd in parables; he did not say anything to them without using a parable." Matthew 13:30, 34

Lesson 135 Part 3: The Parable of the Weeds
Matthew 13:30, 34

Name:

Penmanship Performance: Using the copy your teacher gives you, write the parable in your best cursive handwriting. *This lesson is continued on the next page.*

Lesson 135

The Parable of the Weeds
Part 3 — Matthew 13:30, 34

Name: _____

What does this part of the parable mean to you?

Lesson 136 — The Parable of the Weeds, Part 4

Matthew 13:36b–39

Name:

Cursive Practice: Trace and write the words on the lines. Define each word or use it in a sentence.

Jesus

disciples

Explain

field

answered

sowed

Son of Man

world

kingdom

devil

age

angels

Horizons Penmanship Grade Four 175

Lesson 137 — The Parable of the Weeds, Part 4
Matthew 13:36b–39

Name:

Cursive Practice: Use the blank lines to answer the questions.

What did the disciples ask Jesus to do?

Who is the sower in this parable?

Who is the enemy in this parable?

What is the harvest in this parable?

Who are the harvesters in this parable?

Lesson 138 — The Parable of the Weeds
Part 4 — Matthew 13:36b–39

Name: _____

Manuscript Practice: Use the blank lines to practice writing the parable.

His disciples came to him and said, "Explain to us the parable of the weeds in the field."

He answered: "The one who sowed the good seed is the Son of Man. The field is the world, and the good seed stands for the sons of the kingdom.

The weeds are the sons of the evil one, and the enemy who sows them is the devil.

The harvest is the end of the age, and the harvesters are angels." Matthew 13:36b–39

Lesson 139 — The Parable of the Weeds, Part 4

Matthew 13:36b-39

Name:

Final Cursive Practice: Practice writing the parable on the lines below.

"His disciples came to him and said, 'Explain to us the parable of the weeds in the field.'"

"He answered: 'The one who sowed the good seed is the Son of Man. The field is the world, and the good seed stands for the sons of the kingdom. The weeds are the sons of the evil one, and the enemy who sows them is the devil. The harvest is the end of the age, and the harvesters are angels.'"

Matthew 13:36b-39

Lesson 140

The Parable of the Weeds
Part 4
Matthew 13:36b–39

Name: _____

Penmanship Performance: Using the copy your teacher gives you, write the parable in your best cursive handwriting. *This lesson is continued on the next page.*

Horizons Penmanship Grade Four

Lesson 140 — The Parable of the Weeds, Part 4
Matthew 13:36b–39

Name:

What does this part of the parable mean to you?

Lesson 141: The Parable of the Weeds — Conclusion
Matthew 13:40–43

Name: _____

Cursive Practice: Trace and write the words on the lines. Define each word or use it in a sentence.

fiery

furnace

gnashing

teeth

shine

kingdom

everything

causes

evil

weeping

righteous

Father

Lesson 142 —  The Parable of the Weeds Conclusion — Matthew 13:40–43

Name: _____

Cursive Practice: Use the blank lines to answer the questions.

What happens to the weeds?

Who will the Son of Man send out?

What will they do?

What will the righteous do?

182

Horizons Penmanship 4

Lesson 143: The Parable of the Weeds — Conclusion
Matthew 13:40–43

Name: _____

Manuscript Practice: Use the blank lines to practice writing the parable.

"As the weeds are pulled up and burned in the fire, so it will be at the end of the age. The Son of Man will send out his angels, and they will weed out of his kingdom everything that causes sin and all who do evil.

They will throw them into the fiery furnace where there will be weeping and gnashing of teeth. Then the righteous will shine like the sun in the kingdom of their Father. He who has ears, let him hear." Matthew 13:40–43

Lesson 144 — The Parable of the Weeds Conclusion — Matthew 13:40–43

Name: _____

Final Cursive Practice: Practice writing the parable on the lines below.

"As the weeds are pulled up and burned in the fire, so it will be at the end of the age. The Son of Man will send out his angels, and they will weed out of his kingdom everything that causes sin and all who do evil. They will throw them into the fiery furnace, where there will be weeping and gnashing of teeth. Then the righteous will shine like the sun in the kingdom of their Father. He who has ears, let him hear."

Matthew 13:40–43

Lesson 145: The Parable of the Weeds Conclusion
Matthew 13:40–43

Name: _____

Penmanship Performance: Using the copy your teacher gives you, write the parable in your best cursive handwriting. *This lesson is continued on the next page.*

Horizons Penmanship Grade Four

Lesson 145: The Parable of the Weeds Conclusion
Matthew 13:40–43

What does this part of the parable mean to you?

Lesson 146: The Parable of the Unmerciful Servant, Part 1
Matthew 18:23–27

Name: _____

Cursive Practice: Trace and write the words on the lines. Define each word or use it in a sentence.

The Unmerciful Servant

Therefore

accounts

settlement

thousand

talents

children

debt

patient

master

pity

camels

Horizons Penmanship Grade Four

Lesson 147: The Parable of the Unmerciful Servant, Part 1
Matthew 18:23–27

Name: _____

Cursive Practice: Use the blank lines to answer the questions.

To what does Jesus compare the kingdom of heaven in this parable?

How much did the servant owe his master?

Could the man pay his debt?

What was the master going to do to the man?

Lesson 148: The Parable of the Unmerciful Servant, Part 1

Matthew 18:23–27

Name: _____

Manuscript Practice: Use the blank lines to practice writing the parable.
This lesson is continued on the next page.

The Unmerciful Servant

Jesus said: "Therefore, the kingdom of heaven is like a king who wanted to settle accounts with his servants. As he began the settlement, a man who owed him ten thousand talents was brought to him. Since he was not able to pay, the master ordered that he and his wife and his children and all that he had be sold to repay the debt.

Lesson 148: The Parable of the Unmerciful Servant, Part 1 — Matthew 18:23–27

Name: _____

"The servant fell on his knees before him. 'Be patient with me,' he begged, 'and I will pay back everything.' The servant's master took pity on him, canceled the debt and let him go." Matthew 18:23–27

You may decorate this page with a drawing of your own:

Lesson 149: The Parable of the Unmerciful Servant, Part 1

Matthew 18:23–27

Name: _____

Final Cursive Practice: Use the blank lines to practice writing the parable. *This lesson is continued on the next page.*

The Unmerciful Servant

Jesus said: "Therefore the kingdom of heaven is like a king who wanted to settle accounts with his servants. As he began the settlement, a man who owed him ten thousand talents was brought to him. Since he was not able to pay, the master ordered that he and his wife and his children and all that he had be sold to repay the debt."

Lesson 149 — The Parable of the Unmerciful Servant, Part 1
Matthew 18:23–27

Name: _____

You may decorate this page with a drawing of your own:

"The servant fell on his knees before him. 'Be patient with me,' he begged, 'and I will pay back everything.' The servant's master took pity on him, canceled the debt and let him go." Matthew 18:23–27

Lesson 150 — The Parable of the Unmerciful Servant, Part 1 — Matthew 18:23–27

Name: _____

Penmanship Performance: Using the copy your teacher gives you, write the parable in your best cursive handwriting. *This lesson is continued on the next page.*

Lesson 150: The Parable of the Unmerciful Servant, Part 1
Matthew 18:23–27

Name: _____

What does this part of the parable mean to you?

Lesson 151: The Parable of the Unmerciful Servant, Part 2 (Matthew 18:28–30)

Name: _____

Cursive Practice: Trace and write the words on the lines. Define each word or use it in a sentence.

fellow

hundred

denrii

grabbed

choke

demanded

owe

knees

begged

refused

instead

prison

Horizons Penmanship Grade Four

Lesson 152 — The Parable of the Unmerciful Servant, Part 2, Matthew 18:28–30

Name: _____

Cursive Practice: Use the blank lines to answer the questions.

How much did his fellow servant owe the first servant?

_____
_____
_____

What did the first servant do to his fellow servant?

_____
_____
_____

What did the fellow servant ask when he fell to his knees?

_____
_____
_____

Did the man listen? What did he do?

_____
_____
_____
_____

Lesson 153: The Parable of the Unmerciful Servant, Part 2

Matthew 18:28–30

Name: _____

Manuscript Practice: Use the blank lines to practice writing the parable.

"But when that servant went out, he found one of his fellow servants who owed him a hundred denarii. He grabbed him and began to choke him. 'Pay back what you owe me!' he demanded.

"His fellow servant fell to his knees and begged him, 'Be patient with me, and I will pay you back.'

"But he refused. Instead, he went off and had the man thrown into prison until he could pay the debt."

Matthew 18:28–30

Name:

Final Cursive Practice: Practice writing the parable on the lines below.

"But when that servant went out, he found one of his fellow servants who owed him a hundred denarii. 'Pay back what you owe me!' he demanded."

"His fellow servant fell to his knees and begged him, 'Be patient with me, and I will pay you back.'"

"But he refused. Instead, he went off and had the man thrown into prison until he could pay the debt." Matthew 18:28-30

Lesson 155 — The Parable of the Unmerciful Servant, Part 2
Matthew 18:28–30

Name: _____

Penmanship Performance: Using the copy your teacher gives you, write the parable in your best cursive handwriting. *This lesson is continued on the next page.*

Horizons Penmanship Grade Four

Lesson 155: The Parable of the Unmerciful Servant, Part 2
Matthew 18:28–30

Name: _____

What does this part of the parable mean to you?

Lesson 156

The Parable of the Unmerciful Servant Conclusion
Matthew 18:31–35

Name:

Cursive Practice: Trace and write the words on the lines. Define each word or use it in a sentence.

greatly

distressed

happened

wicked

shouldn't

jailers

tortured

unmerciful

heavenly

treat

unless

forgive

Horizons Penmanship Grade Four

Lesson 157 — The Parable of the Unmerciful Servant, Conclusion — Matthew 18:31–35

Cursive Practice: Use the blank lines to answer the questions.

Who went to the master to tell him what had happened?

What did the master do?

What did the master say to the servant?

What did the master do to the unmerciful servant?

Lesson 158: The Parable of the Unmerciful Servant — Conclusion
Matthew 18:31–35

Name: _____

Manuscript Practice: Use the blank lines to practice writing the parable.

"When the other servants saw what had happened, they were greatly distressed and went and told their master everything that had happened.

"Then the master called the servant in. 'You wicked servant,' he said, 'I canceled all your debt because you begged me to. Shouldn't you have mercy on your fellow servant just as I had on you?' In anger his master turned him over to the jailers to be tortured, until he should pay back all he owed. "This is how my heavenly Father will treat each of you unless you forgive your brother from your heart." Matthew 13:31–35

Lesson 159  **Name:**

Final Cursive Practice: Using the copy your teacher gives you, practice writing the parable on the lines below.

You may decorate this page with a drawing of your own:

Horizons Penmanship Grade Four

Lesson 160 — The Parable of the Unmerciful Servant: Conclusion — Matthew 18:31–35

Name: _____

Penmanship Performance: Using the copy your teacher gives you, write the parable in your best cursive handwriting. *This lesson is continued on the next page.*

Horizons Penmanship Grade Four

Name:

What does this part of the parable mean to you?

You may decorate this page with a drawing of your own: